THE ANGER CODE

Everything you need to know about mastering the inner game of anger

TOCHI JAMES

THE ANGER CODE

Understanding and reducing angry outbursts
regardless of how others treat you

THE ANGER CODE

Understanding and reducing angry outbursts regardless of how others treat you

Offered by Tochi James

(+234)816-4181-432

Published at Smashwords

Thank you for downloading this eBook. This book remains the copyrighted property of the author, and may not be redistributed to others for commercial or non-commercial purposes. If you enjoyed this book, please encourage your friends to purchase & download their own copy from their favorite authorized retailer. Thank you for your support.

ISBN: 9780463974612

To Apeh Augustine and Sunday Adeyi:

Thank you for your brotherly presence

INTRODUCTION TO THE ANGER CODE

□Anybody can become angry, that is easy; but to be angry with the right person, and to the right degree, and at the right time, and for the right purpose, and in the right way, that is not within everybody□s power; that is not easy.□ □ Aristotle

TABLE OF CONTENTS

PART I

UNDERSTANDING ANGER

You don□t know enough
to be angry

1.0 UNDERSTANDING ANGER

The afternoon where it all began

Nothing could explain it. It was on a Thursday afternoon. The kids were packing up to leave the learning premises. Some, were already on their way home, and others, wandered drudgingly past the reception's hallway as they aimed for the exit gate. Two young instructors were sitting at the hallway. One of the young men was excited and exhausted altogether. He had just returned from a gathering of games-loving teenagers. The other handsome, dark skinned educator, sat calm, as passers-by crusaded past the side of their legs. The sun was still shining in her strength, when suddenly, a tall, fair, under 17 years boy let out.

The words of the student spiraled round the head of the light-skinned instructor. Immediately, he summoned the youth to their side. His happy countenance began changing; eyes began flaming danger; blood began pumping faster; muscles began contracting harder; and the amygdala, fully in control. In a twinkle, his hand was over the poor kid. His colleagues tried to halt him, but he persisted, saying, '*I am not angry...*' The more he assured himself with his illusive phrases, the higher his rage intensified. He thought he was in control of his senses, but the ignorant blather didn't realize that he was in a state of mild insanity. They tried to hinder him to a halt, but his **executive brain** was already flooded with that hormone for his present action.

After a while, he stopped. But, the *good venom* stayed in his body system for a great while, before finally calming down.

(This is strange.)

How would an individual shift in a flash, from being happy to becoming madly angry?

(See page <u>here</u> for details □ <u>The Mind Nature of Anger</u>)

FACTS OF ANGER

(1). Anger is Normal
(2). Anger is Empty
(3). Anger is Energy
(4). Anger is You

NORMAL

To be angry is not inhuman: it is absolutely natural for you to react in an unfriendly way to triggers that offend you. When someone breaks your $200 smart phone, it is not unusual for you to flare up at the person. Your outburst of displeasure is what most people would do because whatever doesn□t pleases uses, threatens us. Is being angry then acceptable?

Anger is not positive neither is it negative. It is our responses and reactions to events that are either healthy or unhealthy. The angry person must not condemn herself for being that way, for it is in her nature to get angry. Like anger, love has her consequences. However, what she must lay to heart is this: does she have the strength to live with the consequences of her getting angry.

Many an article, have been written on the effects of angry outbursts, making it appear evil. Nevertheless, not many mortals have been flooded with the ray of the knowledge of anger as a useful and needed make-up of man. Anger, is not an organ in the body you must uproot or destroy; for to do so, is to cease being human. It is your responses and reactions to your seed of anger that are of relevant interest and not your elimination of it.

EMPTY

Nobody ever became angry because of nothing! An event, a circumstance, a thought, or a person, had caused the inflammation of their angry feelings.

Just as nothing happens of itself, likewise, anger is empty of a separate self. For example, a laptop: this is composed of keyboard pads, motherboard, battery, microchips, ics and other useful components, without which the laptop cannot be. For the **Laptop** to be laptop, it needs all those components to exist as one. These components are called elements of the laptop.

In retrospect, also, anger won□t be known as anger without its elements, which we call triggers. These elements are the reasons for you becoming angry. (More would be said of anger triggers in later sections of this book)

ENERGY

All emotion is energy □ Energy without which we would function ineffectively. We are emotional beings. The word emotion is transcribed '*energy* in motion.'

We interact with other forms of energy in the universe because of our energetic design. In addition, we experience a release of an energetic wave when we interact with fellow humans. And yet, it is this wave that makes others vibrate to our frequencies when we become angry.

YOU

If you don't want to see anger, it means you don't want to see who is becoming angry. Then, where is your anger coming from? Who is becoming angry?

I believe you know the answers to those questions, don't you?

STATES OF EXPRESSIONS

There are two states of expressions when we become angry:

(1). Responsive State
(2). Reactive State

Response State

This zone is called the Conscious state. It means you are aware, normal, and in the right frame of mind when you respond to anger triggers. But, this expressive behavior is based on your beliefs about life, your culture beliefs, religious beliefs, and your strong attachment to things.

Also, your perception of events affect your responses: your past encounters, and the way others treated you in the past. The meaning you give or have given to the events of your life would influence how well you respond to anger ☐ because, you are basing your responses on the narratives from your past.

Reaction State

This state is highly biological; and it is called the Unconscious state. In this mode, the amygdala is fully in control, and you are not completely in your right □*thinking senses*□ when you take actions towards anger triggers.

What causes this autopilot response?

(See the page on the **Biology of Anger** for the causes of the reactive state)

LEVELS OF ANGER

Mr. David□s funny statement

A tall suited robust man, with another tall, lanky, low rank police officer, walked into the citadel through the small gate, opposite the road where he parked his car. Many eyes flashed the robust figure as he entourage himself with his security. The on-lookers in their wonder and bewilderment couldn□t seem to uncover the entrants□ assignment, as they remained clueless to his mission with the Nigerian Police Officer. After a while of waiting outside the principal□s office, he stepped in with his Officer for another time of waiting □ I meant talking time.

After spending some many minutes in the principal□s office, another prominent member of the school board was invited in, and then, my humble self, summoned afterwards. The parent of the boy standing on the far end of the right, beside the door, was sitting across from the principal while his escort stood beside him. When I came in, I took a careful glance at the elders present, and greeted.

Already, I knew why I had been summoned. So I wasn□t in a state of shock, neither was I glad about the expected summon. The Principal posed a question to me before the hearers, an answer, which I didn□t fail to provide. And before I could finish my defensive script, another colleague of mine was invited: since he was also involved in the scene that was filed before them.

After much deliberation to resolve the unsettled matter, the Parent decided to wheel us to the police station. As we all stepped our foot outside the Principal□s doorframe, students started nudging their heads from out the windows and doorways of their classes, hoping to catch a glimpse of the young instructors as the policeman wheel them away. When we got to the car outside the gate, neighboring residents also, abandoned their tasks briefly, to satisfy their curiosity of our story as they watched us step into the grey colored car. Many thoughts crossed their minds for the intent by which we were accosted by the Officer: but thankfully, we weren□t handcuffed.

Over at the police station, the principal and the other superior came over to aid us. But it appeared they had showed up a little late, as the matter had long been resolved by a higher rank Police Officer. However, I thanked them for showing up, and we journeyed back to the school.

I wasn□t surprised when a meeting was called upon for the staff: for we all expected it. As at the period of this event, I have never consciously for once being to the Police Station, except for these reasons: first, to report a case of unsatisfied service rendered; and secondly, for angry outburst. During our round-table talk with the Principal, that was where Mr.

David blurted, *"...We all have a level of madness inside of us*☐☐ His statement amused the house, but it was coated with an element of truth that we couldn☐t stash away.

In conclusion, for the remaining scenes of the story, don☐t expect to ask me how it ended, for it was a tragicomedy!

<u>The Levels</u>

Everyone possesses some degree of anger in him or her. The levels of anger ascend the scale □ the lower scales are gradually gaining potentiation, while the higher scales are at their peaks. People flare into rage whenever being triggered; and the inability to restrain unhealthy behavior is a result of long term potentiation (LTD).

This is the reason why an individual operating in the lower level scale of anger will see another reacting furiously to an event, and would be like, □*why is he acting that way?*□

The table below shows the anger levels of individuals:

Very Low	Low	Normal	High	Very High
Rarely shouts	Rarely shouts	Occasionally shouts but not abusively	Shouts abusively	Fights and beats others
Smiles	Show facial displeasure	Frequently reacts but not destructively	Withdraw from others and promotes malice	Destroy things
Gives no place for retaliation	Engages the mirror neurons			Commit murder and suicide
Let go off immediately of triggers	Focuses on the bigger picture			*This Level is highly dangerous and is need of a therapist
Engages the mirror neurons	*This individual is calm			
Focuses on the bigger picture				
*This Level takes a lot of practice and willingness to stay calm				

Did you notice the trend? Very high is at the highest, and very low is at the lowest. This signifies that very high, and high have a strong neural connection (Long Term Potentiation □ LTP). Whereas the others, weak LTP. In order to control your rage, you must go down the scale; and going down is called Depression. This depression is not associated with mood; rather, it means a weakening of strong neural connections in the brain. By making the connections in your brain weaker, you reach the bottom level of the scale (Long Term Depression □ LTD). This makes you less responsive to anger triggers, and puts you in control of your actions.

How do you then cause a LTD? This would be covered in the other sections of this book.

Definition I

Angry expression is a hormonal discharged that is normal based on stressful event, triggered by an external factor.

2.0.   THE BIOLOGY OF ANGER

Who summoned them?

Ggagan, gbagan, was the sound that redounded from the
metal-cone wooden handle bell, mastered by a kid
□ □*assembly,* □ the adolescent called aloud. Everyone□s
attention has been brought to halt, and none even dared asked
who it was that had bade the breathing mortals □ All they
could do was respond to the clarion call; even the adults
weren□t spared by the summoning of the kid.

Before then, at around 7:20am, a flock of homo-sapiens
danced alike in same direction, passing through the inter-
locked floor, smiling at one another along with their lunch
boxes and school bags, as they hurried off to their learning
cages with windows. □*How far,...good morning,* □*how are
you,* □*how about?...*' were the common phrases that flew out
from their oesophagus. They couldn□t help but appear in
their code colour of white tops, and grey downs, as they
motioned breathless in batches under the morning clouds,
like ready soldiers waiting for a dismal command.

Finally, the Principal relieved the students of their standing
duty and they all retired to their window blocks □ not
excluding the teachers. Some minutes later, a female
instructor summoned a group of students into the staff
quarters. Upon their soon, immediate arrival, they ignored

the sight of two sleeping grow-ups African Negros. "Miss Joy□ Miss Joy...," was all that filled their consciousness as they drew closer to her desk with their pending matters. Along in their hands were writing materials □ hoping in anticipation that their complaints would be resolved.

Other members of the staff seem not to care about the invaders presence as their buttocks kissed their seats; and skulls, buried beneath pending tasks in front of their wooden desks. Gradually, the students□ subtle chattering scaled up the roof like an unarranged symphony. □*Get out*□ *are you stupid,* □ were the ear-splitting words that dumbstruck everyone present in the room. The ranter continued, *'Who is bringing all these kids here?*□ A question nobody deemed worthy to answer as they all behold the crier from off their desks in bewilderment. Before any mortal could attempt solving the mysterious question posed, the kids had already fled for survival upon seeing the fury rage countenance of the now standing - Mr. Gongo.

Mr. Feronmi who had one of his legs on his table as he snored, was also awakened from the dead by his partner□s strident crime. This startled the Writer, and he thought, □*what could be the difference between Mr. Gongo and Mr. Feronmi.*□ He prodded further, □*is it genetic, a programming or habitual?*□ all of which he was left to unmask for himself.

The room had gone quiet, with Mr. Gongo seated back in his former position deprived of any further nap. The staff wondered at what they had just experienced, and remained speechless of the scene. All staring eyes shifted from the blaring ranter back to their abandoned tasks. Before any could recover from where they had left off, another comely talker uttered, □*Probably, Mr. Gongo was trying to receive some cash in his dream before the students interrupted.*□ Now, it seemed as if the new speech has made the room more gravy, as they all fastened their gaze at the new speaker as if to be saying, □*Are you okay?'* Before anyone could pass further facial judgment on the last speech made by the Writer, mild laughter resurrected from Mr. Caleb, and the other staff followed suit, faking a smile □ not excluding the loud ranter himself.

And for the question asked, please don□t ask me the answer.

What we learnt from this experience?

(1). Two individuals, same experience, but different reactions.
(2). It simply meant that something was wrong. Not with the situation but with Mr. Gongo since Mr. Feronmi reacted differently.
(3). Mr. Gongo is having an issue with anger.

THE ANGRY BRAIN

The brain is a three-pound device with over 100 billion neurons; and more are still being formed (neurogenesis). The neurons in the brain are interconnected and acts as message carriers and transferors of information from one neuron (pre-synapse) to another neuron (post-synapse). The gap region between a pre-synaptic cell and post-synaptic is called a **synapse**. This is where hormones are released.

The hormones found in the brain are called □ **Neurotransmitters.**

There are two major kinds of brain hormones, we have:

(1). Excitatory Neurotransmitter
(2). Inhibitory Neurotransmitter

Excitatory Neurotransmitter	Inhibitory Neurotransmitter
Causes excitement	Causes calmness
Major excitatory neurotransmitter is Glutamate (about 90%...)	Major inhibitory neurotransmitter is GABA (Gamma Amino Butyric Acid)
Others include: adrenalin, noradrenalin, dopamine	Others include: serotonin, melatonin

What causes our brain to become angry?

One of the key events that cause us to get angry is:

STRESS

High level of stress causes a high-level release of adrenalin, which in turn bypasses the HPA-axis (Hypothalamic-Pituitary-Adrenal), releasing cortisol into the brain. When this is released, it causes a flood over the prefrontal cortex (The executive brain) which is there to help you think clearly. This cortisol release causes a cloudy focus, and that is why if an external factor triggers you or violate your expectations, you tend to react beastly without first thinking of the consequences of your actions. At this stage, the amygdala is overshadowing your thinking zone □ the executive brain; and only in a state of mindfulness would you be restored back to normalcy.

<u>**Neuroplasticity and your Habitual Reponses.**</u>

Don□t wake me

He is a master when it comes to helping mortals gain knowledge. A young, tall, handsome, and potbellied man, married to a fair pretty jewel from the southwestern region of Nigeria. The kids in his school cheered him; and even the guardians of the students loud his praise. He was born a Yoruba citizen, but had grown fond of English as a second tongue. Mr. Kola□s colleagues and friends liked hanging around him, for he had earned the testimony of being a generous giver and a nice soul. However, there was a side of him all wished they never aroused.

One sunny afternoon, after going from door to door, sharing his insights to his young disciples, he retired to the staff quarters and reclined backward, towards the chair behind him for a rest. Kola would not jeopardize this dreamy moment for what he considered trivial. He had barely satisfied his mind exploration when some students on white top uniforms entered the room. They had been summoned by his colleague without his unneeded consent.

The invitees talked to one another as they came into the room, and uttered words before their inviter that no one cared to poke nose. The next scene everyone saw was the head of

Mr. Kola gradually rising from off the desk in front of him. What looked like a full bath of fear, gripped the students when they saw the change in his eyeballs and mug. They needed not to consult any adviser, knowing the kind of man he was when distracted on his trip. Like telepathist, they all knew the plan to execute.

□*Are you mad*□ the enraged linguist master blared. Before anyone could defend the presence of the guilty sincere kids, they had already fled like flash from the gaze of wandering eyes. After Mr. Kola has vomited those words, he returned his head back facing the desk to continue his mission where he left off.

However, he was known for that kind of reaction whenever a supposed noise woke him. It has become a habitual style that even his students aren□t shocked by when he reacts.

In conclusion, please don□t ask me if he was still cheered by his students because he was, and rated one of their favorites too!

HABIT

The brain have the ability to form new neural connections, when learning a skill or forming a habit. Neuron that wire (arrange/connect) together, fire together.

How then is habit formed? It is formed through a continuous wiring of particular neurons in the brain, which strengthens neural connections. If every time you get annoyed, you respond always in an unhealthy way, you will be building and strengthening a particular connection in your brain. A time would come where you would not have to think about your response, you would just react in an autopilot. If the habit is prolonged, it may lead to mental disorder.

How did you learn to say 1+1 = 2, or spell the word □BOY,□ it was through continuous repetitions.

Consequentially, it therefore means that, repetition enhances strong neural connections, which in turn leads to habit. If a negative habitual response is the case, it has become a disorder (mental), which may not be healthy for you and others.

GENETIC CODE

As you may have heard, traits are transferable from ancestors (parents). If either of your parent was the angry type, and the trait was passed down to you, it means that you will likely be vulnerable to responding in an unhealthy way when triggered. However, this DNA trait doesn□t make us victims or mean that we are helpless, rather, it means that we are more prone to responding or reacting in similar manner like our predecessors.

This cycle (trait) can be controlled, broken, or changed, as to the extent that we become aware of our state. With the determination, the willingness to act differently, and a believe that a change would happen, it would.

BRAIN DAMAGE

When there is growth or lesion in any part of the brain, like the Ventromedial Prefrontal Cortex (VMPF), it alters the normal functioning of the brain. That is why you see individuals sometimes, acting in various ways that surprises you. It may be an adult displaying a childish behavior; a kid acting in an unthinkable manner; or people expressing out as if they are insane. When people act out in this condition, you might be forced to ask the question: *Is this person sane?*

No.

Yes. They are not mad or foolish; there is a possibility that they are having a lesion in their brain. Once you understand this, you would begin to look at the world differently; withhold judgments often; and ultimately, weigh possibilities before reacting in an unhealthy manner towards others.

Definition II

Anger expression is a hormonal discharge that is normal based on personal values, triggered by an internal or external factor.

3.0. THE MIND NATURE OF ANGER

Alone in the dark

At first, all I wanted to do, was to satisfy my curiosity. So, I stayed up longer, then a little longer; and when it became glaring that the night was falling fast on me, I resigned my quest. I packed up my materials, locked the door of the library, and left her premises. Everyone had left the school; leaving me alone with some familiar, small, crawling reptiles; gang of annoying mosquitoes; and the male-guard of the organization to keep watch. I could have at least waited to finish my never-ending mission but; the clouds announced a change: a call, which I couldn□t refute.

While I walked home along with my multi-colored bag, and pondered on the matter that lay unresolved, I brooded over on the hormone; and my subconscious threw questions at me, hoping to receive no clear answers. I had read some, and researched broadly, materials on the neurotransmitter but; the adrenalin hormone section seemed to be concealing its mystery from me. This is the hormone responsible for our focus, attention, and also the hormone activated when we become aggressive: how could this ever be, was my myopic bemusement of the matter. Like me, any newbie and older seekers would seek clarification. These were my thoughts: if the adrenalin hormone is responsible for our attention and focus, and aggression, it means removing the hormone would help us feel less aggressive or not aggressive at all. But, if it were to be eliminated, then it means we wouldn☐t be able to exercise our focus effectively! Then, the deduction was, adrenalin isn☐t the problem; for we need the neurotransmitter for our survival. *Then what is the problem?*

Having read different material on the management of anger to the neurology of anger, yet, my curiosity wasn☐t satisfied: though, suggestions were proposed by the authors but, it seemed not to connect with my unknown reason of dissatisfaction. The solutions they proffered were more biologically inclined, as described in the previous pages; which leaves us at the mercy of the factors. However, as I walked in the dark narrow road, which led to a major road, I asked within; and an insight erupted from what I sensed to be the Super-conscious. And then, it felt as if a clouded wall of darkness were dissolved: I paid attention to the insight, and rays of light of clarification fecundated my understanding. Then, suddenly, the awaited answer revealed itself: **Perception** ☐ our explanation of events.

Anger takes it nature form based on our interpretation of the events of life. The meaning you give to any event would determine your response afterwards.

Look at the following images and tell me what you observed.

Do you see a young beautiful lady or an old woman?

**Nothing moves on the page, but you perceive motion.
Rotating Snakes illusion by Akiyoshi Kitaoka.**

Perception is the starting point of any angry outburst.

<u>Note:</u>

Sometimes, the adrenaline hormone is released when we are in a state of excitement, and learning. It means an individual who has been happy, can make a sudden shift to becoming angry. This is as a result of the hormone already released.

So when you are beaming with excitements, also know that you are prone to flaring up in that moment if a trigger arouses your anger seed. Nevertheless, with an understanding of this, you would be able to control your responses and reactions, in order not to act out unhealthily when in excitement.

TRIGGER

A trigger can be any event or condition that violates our peace or expectation.
The hormone being released when we get angry is the same hormone (noradrenalin) being released when we are focused on learning something new or paying attention to a something relevant. However, different neuronal pathways of the adrenergic system are engaged for the intended purpose of either learning something or getting angry. Therefore, this simply means that the hormone (noradrenalin) isn□t the problem: for it is needed for our survival. The problem lies in our values; and our values allow the neurotransmitter to exhibit a nature of anger.

This discovery is not limited to anger as an emotion; it is also true for other emotions. The interpretation we give to events, allow our emotions to transform into different natures like that of a Chameleon: this doesn□t leave us at the mercy of reactions, but allow us to engineer our own responses.

(1). Thoughts create expectations
(2). Beliefs create experiences
(3). Values create expressions

ANGER
HORMONAL DISCHARGE
NATURE TRANSFORM
PERSONAL VALUES
TRIGGER

4.0. ANGER NETWORK

The networks of anger are the root causes responsible for our healthy outburst.

(1). Personal Values
(2). Stress
(3). Genetic Code
(4). Trapped Emotions

PERSONAL VALUES

(i). Beliefs
(ii). Frustration
(iii). Culture
(iv). Disappointment
(v). Perceptions
(vi). Lack of fulfillment
(vii). Interpretation
(viii). Sickness
(ix). Expectation
(x). Fear & worry of the future

Note:

Sometimes, our personal value goes way beyond our beliefs. It extends down to our **Pride of social class**. When our position of office, respect, or the titles people fail to address us by is violated, we become angry. These have nothing to do with others triggering us, but we are the ones who have conditioned ourselves to be offended by the values we have castle up.

(For notes on Stress and Genetic Code, check the page on **Biology of Anger**)

TRAPPED EMOTION

Trapped emotion as the name states, is the emotion trauma that was experienced in the past, and not transformed or released into other forms of energy. This energy motion becomes locked up within us, and make us more vulnerable to responding unhealthy even without our being aware of it cause. It may have become trapped in in our growing up years. Until it is released or transformed, we would still be responding unhealthily.

Past Events = Trapped Emotion

Any of these could the reasons for our trapped emotions:

(i). Loss of loved ones
(ii). Failure
(iii). False actuation
(iv). Humiliation
(v). Shame, disgrace
(vi). Broken relationship
(vii). Maltreatment

(viii). Unfair judgment
(ix). No love/attention

(For further readings on trapped emotions, consult Bradley
Nelson□s book □ *The Emotion Code*)

PART II

THE
EFFECTS

5.0.   ANGER AND YOUR HEALTH

Well-being is a result of balance in the body. When there is imbalance, there would be dis-ease. The human body consists of over 50 trillion of cells that are intelligent. These cells function in two ways:

(1). Growth
(2). Protection

When cells aren't in growth mode, they are in protection mode; and in protection mode, the body becomes vulnerable to sickness. Our cells go into this protection mode when we are angry, fearful, worrisome and expressing other unhealthy emotions.

In addition, when you are going through stress and the stress hormone is being released, the immune system is shut off, thereby exposing the body to internal threats. Also to that, when you become angry, your heart goes from pumping blood at 4litres/min to about 20litres/min: this causes a risk of heart attack which is 8.5 times higher within the 2hours of intense anger outburst.

Likewise, the risk of getting a stroke rises by about 3 times within the 2hours of angry outburst. These vulnerabilities are not abstract statements: for research has shown those to be valid.

<u>Summary</u>

(i). Immune system shut down
(ii). Heart attack risk
(iii). Stroke risk

6.0. ANGER AND YOUR RELATIONSHIPS

RESPONSE is the key factor of any growing or dying relationship.

Do you really know why relationships suffer much damage than necessary? It is because the other party doesn□t know how to respond (I mean to suffer).

If you don□t know how to suffer less, you are more likely to make the other person (the trigger man) suffer more, and also increase your own sufferings. You may think that you are trying to relieve yourself, but in the actual sense of it, you are amplifying your own suffering.

Offenses would definitely come; it would be practically impossible for triggers not to show up. Rather, your knowledgeable response to offensive events is the key to suffering less and sustaining healthy relationship.

Look at it this way □ the person triggering your anger is the one who comes with firewood and kerosene, and you are the one with the matches□ box. What does this mean? It means that you are the master in your relationships. You either strike the matchstick or not. If you do, you□ll set the whole house on fire, and there would be a great damage. However, if you choose not to light the fire, the firewood will be taken out, and communication would be restored.

Some of us have firewood and kerosene, while some of us are in possession of the matches□ box. Rather, should I say that we have both arsenals within us and it all depends on the situation we find ourselves □the trigger or the triggered.

Note

Even if you want to correct the trigger people, you don□t have to do it when they have the firewood and kerosene; because it is less unlikely that you might utter a word that would make up the fire and cause the flames to go up. Thich Nhat Hahn revealed, □*Anger is a living thing. It comes up and it needs time to go back down.*□

THE ANGER TRANSFER CHAIN

This is what happens in the ecosystem of humans when we don□t know how to handle the sufferings of anger within us and that of other persons: the flames of anger escalates, and everybody suffers much more.

For instance, let□s look at the situation of this couple:

A man returns home from work, after the stress at the office and the traffic encountered on the way, on entering the house, his wife stops him and utters disappointedly, '*Look at the time you are coming back; you failed again to keep to your promise□, you can□t be trusted.*□ The tired husband who feels too weak to respond, crusades pass his wife as he walks into his room. While on his way to the room, she keeps yelling: and the man who couldn□t hold on any longer, responds angrily, saying, '*Shut up; you ingrate; must I, always have to deal with you before I find peace in this house?*' If this explosive argument continues, both partners will suffer immensely.

Let us say that one of their children approaches one of them and say, '*Mom, can you please tell me how to pronounce this word?*□ Because her mother doesn□t know how to suffer less, she yells at her daughter, saying, '*Don□t disturb me; go and meet your daddy!*' If the little child is ignorant on how to suffer less, she goes to school the following day, and finds it difficult concentrating in class: because she has been affected psychologically. She will nurture the thoughts: *mummy doesn□t care; she doesn□t love me*□ and so on. Gradually, as this continues, she would start developing □**Attention Deficit Disorder.**□

More so, let us say that her classroom teacher is also ignorant of the □**Anger Code,**' she too, will shout angrily at the poor girl, saying, '*What is wrong with you; why are you not concentrating; you are so dull for my liking.*' Unknown to the good teacher, she makes the girl suffer more: and ignorantly, she suffers too.

This is how the **virus of anger** keeps spreading from one person to another. Some call this virus, the transfer of aggression; and here, we□ll address it as: **the network chain of anger.**

(1). What if the woman knew that her husband was stressed and not in the right frame of mind, would she have reacted differently?
(2). What if she had responded to her husband in knowledge, would she have prevented her kid from suffering psychologically?
(3). What if the teacher at school had understanding of the □*Anger Code*□, would she have made the kid to suffer less.

This ignorance is the reason for intra-communal crises, inter-tribal oppositions, and wars around the world: for the virus keeps spreading between people due to the ignorance among us. However, to end this, you and I must seek first to know and understand the other person, before committing to acting unguided.

Lesson: You don□t know enough to be angry

7.0. ANGER AND PRODUCTIVITY

Whose pen is this?

She was a young, dazzling, and energetic lady from the eastern region of Nigeria. The kids had come to like her despite her early arrival appointment to the school management board. Hardly would a day pass by that you won□t see Miss Kachi laugh out loud; even the staff had grown to appreciate this side of her personality.

After spending some months in the students□ citadel, her keeping to deadlines revealed how industrious she was. However, this was a behavior organizations like the one she worked for weren□t willing to miss.

One sunny afternoon, she walked in from a station point whose exit none intended to verify, and into the staff room, snatched Mr. John□s pen from off his hand where he was sitting. □*Give me the pen*□ the young man pleaded softly. □*This is the pen I got from the principal,'* the lady reacted. □*I am not joking,'* the estranged Music facilitator stressed as he tried to let her know that the pen wasn□t the one she thought of but his.

Notwithstanding, she held to her resolve that the pen was hers; and the debate amplified. Mr. John who was rattled by the situation reacted in a manner that has not been seen of him before: at least not to the new staff. John□s reaction surprised the mortals in the room over Kachi□s defiance.

Eventually, when she discovered the truth about the pen, she felt sorry to have disrupted the bliss among the staff. So, I approached her, *'Apologize to him,'* I advised. Rather, she thought to herself, *'He will get over it.*□ I expanded further to her that Mr. John wouldn□t give 100% concentration into what he was doing at that moment before the pen debate. The Writer made the statement because he knew that angry outburst affected focus and productivity.

Some seconds later, the Music Instructor let out, □*You see, you□ve made me not to concentrate on what I was doing,*□ as if to confirm what has been earlier prophesied. He packed up his materials for a while before starting out again.

In conclusion, don□t ask me if they didn□t make up: because they did!

PRODUCTIVITY

How does anger affect you at the work place? Anger doesn□t change your capacity nor does it reduce your capability, what it does is that it causes a **SHIFTING**.

For instance, when you are driving and your phone rings or you sight an accident, there would be a shifting in your present focus □ so it is with anger. If you aren□t a good practitioner of your emotion, you□ll also be tempted to dwell and focus long on the events that aroused your anger. However, if attention is given to the event of anger, energy would be deployed into thinking about the event, thereby short-circuiting the flow of energy required for other tasks you have set out to accomplish for that day, week or month.

Attention!

When there is a trigger to generate anger in you, it causes a quick shift that creates:

(i). Scattered attention
(ii). Narrowed focus

Attention starts the process of neuroplasticity. Neuroplasticity is a branch in neuroscience that deals with the rewiring of neural networks in the brain. When attention is scattered, it causes a stir in the brain of what to do exactly, and this increases your stress level. □*Should I do this or should I do that* □ this instability of jumping from one thought to another creates imbalance in the brain, indecisiveness, and there wouldn□t be maximum concentration on the task at hand.

The question you are to ask yourself is, □*What am I focusing on at the moment?*□ If your focus is on the event of anger, whatever meaning (perception) you give to it, you□ll feel. And what you feel, you□ll express forward; be it the meaning of disrespect, hurt or anything.

If you are not able to suffer less, the work in your hand will suffer greatly.

Anger-Productivity Reality

(1). Anger causes a shift in focus
(2). Energy is deployed into thinking about anger situation
(3). Work production either grows or suffers
(4). The whole organization suffers
(5). Profit margin is dropped
(6). Customers are either retained or lost
(7). If you suffer, the work suffers; and if the work suffers, you suffer
(8). If you suffer less, your organization suffers less

PART III

THE HEALING

8.0. HEALING

Replace Your Values

Healthy and compassion filled relationships is borne out of the understanding of anger. If you will gain mastery over your expressions, you may have to replace the unhealthy values with healthy ones.

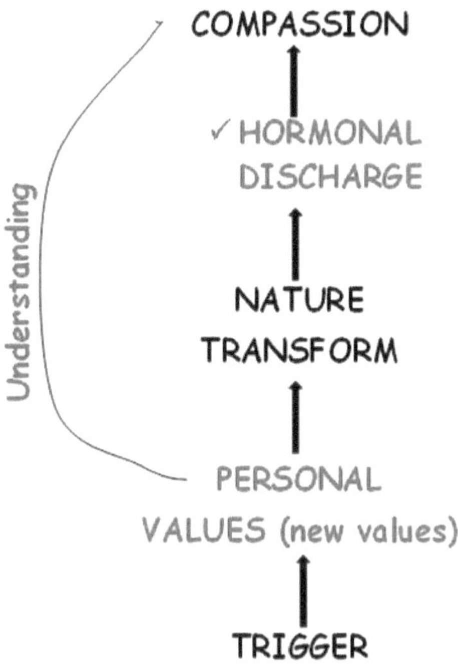

COMPASSION
✓ HORMONAL DISCHARGE
NATURE TRANSFORM
PERSONAL VALUES (new values)
TRIGGER
Understanding

<u>**Know**</u>:

Of all the stages, the only place you really have power over,
is the PERSONAL VALUES zone. You can□t do anything
about the nature of your hormone, neither can you change
other people (external triggers). The only place you wield
influence over, is your VALUES zone

.

MINDFULNESS OF ANGER & STRESS MANAGEMENT

You have to know if you are getting angry habitually whenever a particular trigger is initiated. If that is the case, that your response is a habit, then you'll need to create another neural connection by responding in the way which you would like to see happen. This will be challenging at first, but, it will help rewire your brain, and depress the old neural connection.

Remember these:

(1). What you don't use, you lose
(2). Neurons that wire together, fire together
(3). Repetition breeds habits

STRESS MANANGEMENT

Stress occurs when there is scattered attention and a high level increase of cortisol in the brain.

How to manage stress level:

(i). Have a to-do-list for a day, week, or month, and organize according to priority.
(ii). Shun procrastination. Do what needs to be done today and avoid *carry over* as possible.
(iii). Learn to say no – you can't do everything at the same time.

PROCRASTINATION

The more you keep pushing your work over to another time or day; it keeps piling up and getting much bigger. The day you set out to do the work you have shifted, it will appear overwhelming, and that alone is enough to cause a mad rush release of cortisol into your brain. This could also lead to a sudden breakdown.

A piece of advice:

(i). Take a break for a moment to relax, reflect and renew your mind
(ii). Accept the facts, take responsibility and strategize for change.
(iii). Set up your environment to win (only let those tasks, which you want to do be in front of you or you will be distracted).

<u>Note:</u>
Individuals who don□t know how to manage their own stress level will tend to stress you.

ANGRY PEOPLE

Angry people are not always bad. It is just that the connection of neurons for response to anger is strong (LTP).

When you understand this, you will have compassion on them because they are actually suffering, and don□t know how to end their sufferings. That is why after they might have displayed their rage, they feel ashamed, and sorry for themselves. Likewise, if you keep responding to these people angrily, you would intensify their sufferings.

Remember, your duty is to help others suffer less.

9.0   TECHNIQUES

SEROTONIN

What is serotonin? This is an inhibitory neurotransmitter in the brain. It is known as the *feel-good* hormone, and helps increases our calmness level.

You can calm yourself and increase your serotonin level in several ways:

PRACTICE DEEP/COMPASSIONATE LISTENING

This is the act of just listening for the sake of listening with no intention to judge, comment or label. It is to completely absorbed oneself in others speech.

PRACTICE DEEP BREATHING

This is a process of inhaling and exhaling air. It helps calm the nerves and muscles that have been tensed up by anger.

You can breathe in and hold for at least 3seconds and release. This could be repeated three to four times, or as many times as possible as you wish.

In addition, when practicing this exercise, your focus should be on your breathing and not on other events, for this will enhance the process.

STILLNESS EXERCISE

This is an act of becoming non-responsive and reactive to events that crosses your mind. Why this exercise?

It helps rewire the brain to be non-responsive to anger triggers. You can achieve this by sitting still in a quiet place, and just allowing thoughts to pass through your mind with no intention to contribute, attack, judge or label them. It will help keep your mind, soul, and body calm, by bringing you to the present moment. This could be achieved in about 5mins or more.

AEROBIC EXERCISE

The importance of exercising from anti-ageing, neurogenesis, neuroplasticity, BDNF (Brain Derived Neurotropic Factor) to serotonin increase cannot be overemphasized. Daily exercise practices help increases the serotonin level in the brain, which aids in calming us when we get angry.

EXPOSURE TO NATURAL SUNLIGHT

Research has shown that when we expose ourselves to natural sunlight, our serotonin level rises. In addition, this would help in improving our calmness level.

THE ULTIMATE GAME CHANGER

He that offends not in word is a perfect man and able to bridle the whole body. James 3:2 KJV

Give to Caesar…

It was on a Thursday morning that I had left the house to an undecided location, to study. Passing through the gate of the 5-section detached self-contain behind my shoulders, was a woman carrying a baby. She is my neighbor, and the little boy under her cuddle had long celebrated his arrival into planet earth some months back. I couldn't help but be drawn by the charm of her radiant son, so I turned behind. In a matter of few seconds, I had abandoned my purpose as I approached the family with another mission. She couldn't exact my thoughts of approach until my two hands stretched towards her child. Her face glimmered with a sense of safety as she transferred the dark toddler into my hands. The small boy wasn't numb at his age, as he attempted to grip the white folded, black inked, printed A-4 manuals under my armpit with his mouth. He smiled under my care while all I did was wag my head sideways at him. Not to keep the standing momma waiting forever, I presented the merry boy back into her arms to further caress her son to mirth.

After returning the human back to his owner, I put my leg over, across the $1^{1/2}$ inches pavement that separated my other feet. Now, with my foot on the same-leveled territory, I journeyed forward without mercy, as I matched on the short sprouted weeds around me. On reaching the gate, I faced east and reclaimed my lost call. Soon, I was less than 40 meters distance from my residence on the extreme side of my starting point □ now, under a serene atmosphere. I sat down by the bituminous pavement I found by the side of the road, opened my manuals, and flipped through carefully, as I studied on the science of empathy.

After some seconds of marrying my buttocks to the cemented $1^{1/2}$ inches pavement, I shifted to another section of the slab pavement hoping to find ease. As I studied and pondered, two dark figures approached west from my rear. One would have guessed they were *'Benueians'* (Benue State indigene). Good morning, they chorused. *'Good morning,'* was my warm response. Their foot moved as they greeted. As they intended walking through the woods rightly behind me, I hastily cut-in, □*Is there road here?*□ The elder of the boys replied, *'Yes.'* Really, that was how I felt on the inside. While they explored the woods, I heard the rattling sounds of dried fallen leaves under their energetic steps. I had thought they had come to catch something like insects or gather woods, but neither of those appeared their mission. Still unbothered by their mission statement, I felt drawn by the woods myself, and hastily peeped behind me, looking occasionally at the wind supported trees.

Later, after what seemed like many minutes, I courageously leaped my whole body into the small forest. □*Wow!*□ I expressed within. Barely had I travelled a quarter of the mile when I started helping myself up a tree. Climbing up a tree was something I hadn□t done for years, and there was an opportunity staring before me to have a little fun. Consequentially, my manuals with my cell phone weren□t left behind as I journeyed up the wooden heights. From above the ground, I could feel the warmth welcome of the green leaves, coupled with the pleasant silence of the air that flowed. Notwithstanding, for a few moments, on the tree, I glanced through my materials as if promoting a new way of studying.

After a short while, the joy of being in the woods started waning. I could smell something □ it fumes like dried feaces from □*long ago.*□ The more I tried to withstand the odour, the further I got dissatisfied with the putrid smell resonating from the surface of the fallen leaves. I stood up upright on the tree, feeling uncomfortable with the odd scent, and right there, in that moment, was when I asked the question □ *"What was Jesus□ strategy?"*□

An insight erupted, □*Give unto Caesar what is Caesar□s.*□ I shrugged within and became confused as to how this

statement could be a strategy for controlling anger. As I
wrestle with my thoughts, further insights erupted:

Hush

During Jesus Christ days of trial, He was faced with different
accusations from different faces, and yet was indifferent
towards taking up a defense. His mission was to see that the
people got reconciled to their Creator. Notwithstanding, His
peace was attacked but He kept the peace in Himself to
ensure peace continued. Moreover, He was the price of
peace, how then should He deny himself.

When He was presented with a matter of paying tax, His
response was, *'Give unto Caesar what is Caesar□s.□* There
are times in our lives we just have to let go in situations that
are likely to arouse our anger. Jesus was so clear in His
statement when He told His disciple to let go □ *Give unto
Caesar what is Caesar□s.* His disciple had thought for him
to react to the tax payment but to his surprise, his Master
expressed, □*Let go.*□ Giving to Caesar that which is
Caesar□s, is a principle laid out by Jesus to aid us in
ensuring our state of sanity and serenity in this life.

At another time, when He was accused by the Jews for
heresy and defamation, He kept silent like a sheep heading
for a slaughter. Also, when superior leaders like Pilate
approached Him, He kept quiet. In addition, as if that wasn□t

enough, a fellow condemned, the thief annoyed Him, yet, He still kept his cool.

The experience of Jesus teaches us that □ when people say things either to mock you, cause you or ridicule you, you should keep silent.

Keep Silent

This happens to be one of my favorite techniques, yet most challenging to uphold. Naturally, in the face of a situation, most of us would love to defend ourselves □ it is normal.

However, when it comes to managing our anger and suffering much less, this is an antidote we can□t just ignore.

Looking at the life of Jesus during his tumultuous days, He kept one common denominator alive during his trials □ silence. He wasn□t silent to every statement but, here is what we learnt:

(1). Any said statement to mock Him, ridicule or annoy him□He remained speechless.
(2). Any said statement for insight or to identify His person, He responded wisely.

The next question that comes to mind is this: was He just silent as a statue or was there another activity going on within.

Actually, I suppose He observed the following when He left off answering:

(1). He intentionally ignored the negative statements.
(2). He observed his breath.
(3). He observed the stillness exercise.

This is the one technique that envelops all the other techniques.

Analysis:

If you don□t want to offend in word, it means you□ll either be silent or utter something healthy. Also, if you are silent not wanting to offend, it means you□ll have to listen with compassion; be still; and observe your breath by ignoring the trigger.

10.0 THE ANGER CODES

THE WISDOM OF SILENCE

(i). Never ridicule the wisdom of silence; for it will save you from a lot of messes, and grant you the clarity to see situations for what they really are.

(ii). Sometimes, silence never means weakness □ it is just what you aren□t thinking about.

(iii). No matter how pressured you are to break your silence, remind yourself that: □*It isn□t worth it.*□

(iv). Your words could make you suffer. More so, the words of another can make you suffer; so, you had better choose how much you would like to suffer.

(v). Remember this last one: forgiveness isn□t weakness; letting go isn□t weakness; allowing yourself to be beaten isn□t weakness either, it is a *holy trick* □just for PEACE to reign.

The Anger Code:

You don□t know enough to be angry. Seek first, always to understand before committing to taking action; and never, neglect the knowledge of your own biology.

This book has provided you with some helpful techniques, therefore, use the tools to sharpen, change and help your life. I will see you on the other side of a rich, better, and healthy relationship(s).

Thank you.

REFERENCES

i.   Hanh, T.N. (1988). *The Heart of Understanding.* California: Parallax Press

ii.   Hanh, T.N.(2001). *Anger.* New York: Penguin Putnam Inc.

iii.   Arden J.B. (2010). *Rewire Your Brain.* New Jersey: John Wiley & Sons Inc.

iv.   Nelson B. (2007). *The Emotion Code.* Mesquite, NV: Wellness Unmasked Publishing.

v.   Singer, T. (2008).Understanding Others: brain Mechanisms of Theory of Mind and Empathy. *Neuroeconomics: Decision Making and the Brain,* 249-263

vi.   Perlmutter, D. (2013). Epigenetics as Fuel for Brain *Health. Alternative and Complementary Therapies.*

vii.   Picton, TW, Alain, C, Mcintosh, AR. The Theatre of the Mind: Physiological Studies of the human Frontal Lobe. *Principle of Frontal Lobe function,* 109-123.

viii.   Decety, J. (2010). The Neurodevelopment of Empathy in Humans. *Developmental Neuroscience.*

ix.   Hanson, R. (2007). Empathy (n.d.)

x.   Jerkins, TA, Nguyen, JC, et al. (2016). Influence of Tryptophan and serotonin on Mood and cognition with a Possible role of the Gut-Brain Axis. *Nutrients*

xi.   Rex, A, Fink, H. (). Neurotransmitter and Behaviour: Serotonin and Anxiety. Institute of Pharmacology and Toxicology, School of Veterinary Medicine,Freie Universitat Berlin, Berlin, 19

xii.   Serotonin Levels Affect Brains Response to Anger. (n.d.). Retrieved February 18, 2018. https://www.reuters.com/article/us-serotonin/serotonin-levels-affect-brain□s-response-to-anger

xiii.   Anatomy of the Brain. (n.d.). Retrieved February 18, 2018. https://www.mayfieldclinic.com

xiv.   Arita, H. (2009). Brain Mechanisms of Poor Anger Management. *JMAJ* 52(3): 184-190

xv.   Nutt, D. GABA Receptors: Subtypes, Regional Distribution, and Function. *Journal of Clinical Sleep Medicine.*

xvi.   Mendius, R. (2007). Train your Brain: From Anger to Peace. (n.d.).

xvii.   Slate, M.K. (2017). Neurotransmitters: Their Role in the Body. (n.d.). *RN. ORG*

xviii.   Denning, N. *Angry Brain*

xix.   De Silva, P. (2017). The Body and the Emotions: Anger, Disgust and Contempt. *Emotions and the Body in Buddhist Contemplative Practice and Mindfulness-Based Therapy,* DOI 10.1007/978-3-319-55929-2_2

xx.   Dikrainian, K. (2015). The Amazing Brain. (n.d.). Biological Society of Cell Biology.

xxi.   How Anger Affects your Brain and Body. (n.d.). (2017). The National Institute for the Clinical Application of Behavioral Medicine. www.nicabm.com

xxii.   Bailey, S.J. (2011). Managing Anger for Better Health and Relationships. Montana State University.

xxiii.   Richards, D.A. Your Amazing Brain. (n.d.). www.HaveFunTeaching.com. http://kids.nationalgeographic.com

xxiv.   Wilson R.K. Anger, Fairness and What□s in the Brain. Department of Political Science, Rice University.

xxv.   Scott, S.K.; Sauter, D.A.; McGettigan, C. (2010). Brain Mechanisms for Processing Perceived Emotional Vocalizations in Humans. *Handbook of Mammalian Vocalization: An Integrative Neuroscience Approach.*

xxvi.   Maag, J.W. *Controlling Your Emotions and Behavior Regardless of How Disagreeably Others Treat You.* (n.d.). University of Nebraska-Lincoln, Lincoln, NE

xxvii.   Bartholomew, N.G. & Simpson, D.D. (2005). Understanding and Reducing Angry Feelings. TCU Mapping-Enhanced Counseling Manuals for Adaptive Treatment.

xxviii.   Sarah, P. (2012). *This is Your Brain on Empathy: The Interpersonal neurobiology of Communication.* (n.d.)

xxix.   Hendricks, L.; Bore S.; et al. (2013). The Effects of anger on the Brain and Body. National Forum Journal of Counseling and Addiction, Vol 2 (1)

xxx.   Wagenhals, D. *This is Your Brain on Anger*

xxxi.   Controlling Anger: A Self-help Guide. NHS Foundation Trust.

xxxii.   Lipton B.H. (2007). The Wisdom of Your Cells

xxxiii.   Cool Down: Anger and How to Deal With it. (n.d.). (2008). www.mentalhealth.org.uk Mental Health Foundation, London.

ABOUT THE AUTHOR

Tochi James is an educator. He serves as the Principal Consultant of **Creadents Impressions.**

Connect with Tochi

I really appreciate you reading my book! Here are my social media coordinates:

Friend me on Facebook: http://facebook.com/tochijames100

Follow me on Twitter: http://twitter.com/Tochi_James

Follow me on Instagram: IG: @tochi.james

Favorite my Smashwords author page: https://www.smashwords.com/profile/view/tochijames

Connect on LinkedIn: http://www.linkedin.com/in/tochukwuokoro

Email: tochi789@gmail.com

Enquiry: (+234)816-4181-432